Python Programming for Intermediates

Learn the Fundamentals of Python in 7 Days

By Michael Knapp

Table of Contents

INTRODUCTION

Welcome to this training for the Kindle edition of Python for Intermediates. This book is going to go more in depth than the previous beginner's book did in showing you how you can use Python to its fullest advantage.

In the beginner's book, you learned some of the basic functions of Python and the various pieces of code that you are going to be able to input into Python so that you can make that function work properly. However, in this book, you are going to learn about other functions and pieces of the code that will work with the functions that you already know.

It is here that you are going to be taking another step towards being able to program your own applications, websites, and anything else that you could possibly want to program all with simple blocks of code that you learned from a beginner's book.

Do not rush into thinking that you are going to be able to write your own computer application just yet. That is going to require that you get through this book and the next one to get a complete understanding of how Python works.

The intermediate level is going to be a level that you may think does not need to be explored because some of it may end up being completely irrelevant to what it is that you are going to do with Python. However, you never know what you are going to find in this book that may just make or break the code that you are completing. So, please do not skip over this book thinking that you are not going to learn something new because

I assure you, there is always something new for you to learn even if it is something simple.

You may see some of the same functions that you saw in the previous book; there is no information is going to be repeated between the two books. Instead, you are going to see a new use for that particular function or string of code that you have seen before. This is done because, just like Python, most of what is placed into the program is going to be versatile and not only work in one way for one data type, but a different way for another data type should it be able to be passed between the different types. Some scripts and functions must stick to one specific type so that they work the way that they are supposed to work.

Each section in this book is going to contain examples that are going to show you what the code should look like when you insert it into your own Python program. Do not be upset if your code does not work properly the first time, some of what you are going to learn in here is going to take a moment for you to be able to learn and the more practice that you get, the easier it is going to be for you to understand fully what is going on.

Do not be afraid to go to the Python website if you are in need of some extra help or to have someone explain it to you in a different way. There are plenty of volunteers who work with Python who are willing to help because they are not only trying to get Python to become the chosen programming language, but they want to make sure that it is efficient and user-friendly. What better way to do this than to be available to answer questions and discover what problems the users are having?

Once again, I must reiterate that this book was written for educational purposes only in an effort to help those who would like to learn how to code with Python for personal or professional reasons. While Python has many purposes such as hacking, it is not recommended that you use Python for this purpose unless it is part of your job legally, such as with the government or a company that has hired you to do ethical hacking for them.

In the event that you are doing ethical hacking, keep in mind that you have gotten the proper certification that allows for you to hack without getting into trouble, and with that being said, you should not take any sensitive information that you may get your hands on and use it for your own personal gain. You are being trusted with this information, and you should not break the trust that you have created with your employer.

Those who use hacking for their own gain, no matter what sort of methods you are using, it is highly illegal, and this book is going to stand behind saying that you should not do it. While knowing how to hack is a valuable skill, it is not one that should be used in an effort to sell other people's personal information. Should you get caught by law enforcement, the system administrator, or the government of the area in which you are currently residing, then you are going to be punished according to the laws and regulations that they have set forth. Many times, this is going to include some sort of jail time, a fine, and a mark on your permanent record.

So, once again, please do not use the lessons that are in this book for anything that could be considered illegal. Everything was written with the hopes of making it easier for you to advance in your personal or professional life as well as enable you to have knowledge that a lot of people are not going to possess due to the fact that they believe learning a programming language is too hard or because they do not find it helpful.

With that being said, you are going to be placing yourself above these people and learning something that could assist you in changing the world!

CHAPTER 1: OBJECTS IN PYTHON

An object in Python is considered to be the abstraction that is over any data that you insert into Python. This means that every value is going to have an object attached to it inside of Python. With every object comes an identity, a value, and a type. The identity of the object is never going to change after you have created it. The function id (obj) is going to give you an integer which will then be the representation of that object's identity.

Your 'is' operator will take that identity and compare it to another object's identity effectively returning a Boolean to you. Should you be using the CPython version, then the id () method is going to return an integer that will give you the location as to where the object is located on the memory of Python which will be how you uniquely identify your objects.

This is thought to be an implementation detail that Python is allowed to return any value that it deems fit that will identify the object in a unique way within the interpreter.

In using the type () function, you are also going to get the type of the object returned as an object itself. The object's type is going to be unchangeable typically. But, the type is going to be the determining factor as to what operations that object is going to support as well as define any values that could be tied to that object type.

Being that Python is a dynamic language, types do not have to be associated with a variable. Therefore, the variable of 'q' can refer to strings now and then later in your code, refer to an integer.

Example

Q = 4

A = kiss

Unlike JavaScript, Python is dynamic mostly since it works with an interpreter that is never going to change the type of object that you are working with. Therefore, any actions that you do, like adding a string to a number is going to create an exception in Python.

Example

Q = kiss

Q + 1

Trace (the last call):

File <nidts> line 2, in < tuple >

Type error: unable to convert integer object to str

Also unlike if you were to use this code in JavaScript, with Python, the code will succeed thanks to the interpreter converting the integer into a string so that it can be added to the string that you have already provided.

Python objects are going to have two "settings."

1. Mutable: these objects can be changed by you or the program.

Example

A = [2, 4, 1]

T = [3, 5, 6]

A = a + t

A

[2, 4, 1, 3, 5, 6]

If you have switched to Python from a different programming language, then you are going to probably be scratching your head wondering why objects are mutable. This is because Python has a pass by object reference code written in so that any value for the object is referenced by the values that are passed into the function or even the method by its name and the calls that are tied to the variable. These are going to be considered the reference values.

Example

A

[8, 5, 8]

a and t are going to refer to the same list

T = x

changes done to a are going to be reflected on t

A. Extend ([1, 4, 6])

[8, 5, 8, 1, 4, 6]

Both a and t are going to be referring to the same object, so whenever you change one thing on list a, it is then going to be changed to list t. To fully get this, you must look at the variable of a and know that usually, it is not going to hold the list that it is holding in the example. Instead, it is going to hold the reference to where the object is actually located, then when variable t is bound to any value that is found inside of a, it will too contain a reference to what can be seen in list a.

Whenever an operation is completed on list a, then it is going to also be carried out on list t. Essentially, anything done to one list has to be reflected on the other.

2. Immutable objects: these objects cannot be changed. As you learned in the last book, this is a prime example of what a tuple is. So, at the point in time that it has been created, it cannot be changed for any reason with any sort of code.

Example

A = (3, 4, 5, 6, 7)

A [0]

4

A [0] = 93

Trace (most recent call) :

File <nidts> line 1 in < module >

Type error: your tuple is not going to support this item.

But, immutable objects can hold mutable objects in the event that the mutable object's value has been changed or can be changed despite the fact that it is part of an immutable object.

Example

While a tuple is an immutable object, tuples are going to be comprised of list objects which are mutable. Therefore, any list objects that are in our tuple are going to have be able to be changed.

A = [2, 4, 5, 6]

A = m

A

([2, 4, 5, 6])

A [7]

[2, 4, 5, 6]

A [7]. Append (12)

([2, 4, 5, 6, 12])

Object references both weak and strong

The objects in Python are going to get their reference from the names that they are bound to. The binding is going to come from assigning functions or methods to the objects arguments. These functions and methods will call the bonded object for the argument names.

Each time that a reference is made to an object, the count for the reference will be increased. You will be able to calculate out what the reference count is by using the sys.getrefcount method.

Example

Import sys

A = [ ]

W = a

for this example, there are three references to the list objects. A, w, and the binding that occurred for the object's argument.

Sys. Get recount (a)

3

References can be found as strong or weak. However, when you discuss the references, it is going to be a strong reference that you are going to want your object to point towards. Looking at the example in the previous section, you are going to note that these references are going to be strong.

One of the defining characteristics for creating a strong reference is going to be done whenever the reference count is incremented by one for the reference object. Essentially this means that the trash man is not going to touch that object due to the fact that he is only going to "collect" the objects that have a reference count of zero.

A weak reference is not going to increase the reference count of the object that is being referred to. The weak references are going to use the module weak ref.

Example

Class oops

Pass

A = pass ( )

E = a

Sys. Getrefcount (a)

3

E = weakref. Ref (a)

Sys. Getrefcount (a)

3

L ( )

<_main_. Opps object at 9 a 1932g9382>

Type (l)

<class 'weakref'>

This function is going to give you the result of an object that is going to be called whenever the weak reference object is called.

The module weakref will also work with the code weakref.proxy better than it would if you were to put weakref.ref into your code whenever you are trying to create a weak reference. With the proxy method, a proxy object is going to be created in order to be used with the primary object so that there is no need for a call to be performed.

Example

E = weakref.proxy (n)

E

<weakproxy at 3x93920ib93to oop at 0x123414959>

e. _dict_

{ }

At the point in time that the strong references for any object have been deleted, the weak references are going to lose their references to what the original object was which then makes that object to where it can be collected by the trash man.

Example

Del e

Del f

A

<Weakproxy at 0x03259ba99 to no type at 0x9331049a4>

w. _dict_

trace (to the most recent call):

file "<nidts>" line 2 in <module>

error the reference: weakly- referenced objects that are no longer found

1 ()

1 () ._ dict_

trace (to the most recent call) :

file "<stdin>" line 2 in <module>

error attribute: "no type" object does not include an attribute. '_dict_.'

The hierarchy of data types in Python

You have already learned that Python has a lot of built-in modules and various other tools that you are going to have access to that are going to make your job with Python easier. Well, Python also has types that are built in, and each of those types is going to fall into categories that you need to know when you are working with data types.

None

With this type, there is going to be a single object that contains one value. In order to access this type, the keyword none will be used. The none type is meant to show that there is not a value and most of the time, it will be returned by the functions that are not returning values.

Example

Python

Def print _ cat (cat) :

Print (cat)

cat = print_cat ("scrunchy")

Scrunchy

Cat

Type (cat)

<class 'none type'>

When using the none type your value for your truth will always be returned as false.

Notimplemented

As another single object, single value type, the value of notimplemented is going to be placed into your code so that you invoke the built-in tools that are associated with it. Any object that is returned with this type will only occur whenever you want to delegate a search for any implementation of a method to the interpreter instead of going the traditional route with the notimplementederror.

Example

Class: dog

Def _init_ (own, number) :

Own. Number = number

Def _re_ (own, different) :

Should isinstance (different, dog) :

Print ('comparison of dogs in progress')

Return different. Number == own. Number

Print ('unable to compare the instances')

Return notimplemented

The program may try and make a comparison due to the fact that you have placed it in your code to be executed this way. The effect of using this type is going to be able to be seen clearly. Whenever Python has x = z in the code that it is carrying out, the results are going to be called from x. _ eq _ (z).

Example

X = oops (1)

Y = rub (1)

X == y

Comparing the instance x with instance y

True

X == x

Comparing instance x with instance x

True

Y == y

Comparing instance y with instance y

True

However, what is going to happen whenever you compare these two instances together? Due to the fact that _eq_ () is going to be implemented, the instance variable is going to look at the other argument as if it is an instance of the other object. With that being said, it is going to be handled according to the module that is built into Python which then returns a value of true.

Now, let's look at it as if we turned it around and took our second object and compared it to the first. Whenever the code is invoked, the notimplemented object will be returned due to the fact that the first object can only support the comparison of objects where the first object comes first in the sequence.

Example

Y == x

Cannot one instance of the other class

When comparing instances of y to x

True

In calling the y. _eq_ (x) method, your returned value is going to force the interpreter to invoke the _eq_() method in the value that is listed first. Since this comparison is defined with the method, then you will get a true result.

Notimplemented objects are going to contain a true value.

Ellipsis

The ellipsis type will be another single object single value type. It is with this value that the object is going to be accessed by placing three periods otherwise known as an ellipsis. You can always put the type name in so that it is called on. Your truth for ellipsis values will be true, and you will see that it is mostly going to be used when working with the numeric type when it comes to slicing matrixes and creating indexes. The documentation for numpy will allow you to have more insight as to how this type is going to be used inside of Python.

Numeric

Numeric types are going to be referred to as numbers when you are reading about the various types. They are going to be the few types that we talked about in the beginner's guide but will go over in a little more detail here. Keep in mind that the number objects will be immutable, so after they have been created, they are not going to be able to be changed.

1. Plain integers: a plain integer is going to fall in the range of 2147483647 to – 2147483648 when it is being used on a 32-bit computer. If you are using a larger bit computer, the range is going to be adjusted slightly so you may need to check your word size to know just what the range is. A longer integer is going to be returned whenever an operation is completed, and the answer for it is not inside of the given range. This is going to be the point in time where an overflow error is raised by the program. To make sure the mask and shift operations work, the integer is going to take on the assumption that the binary will have two complement

notations that will be using 32 bits at the very least. It is also going to make sure that all the bits are open for the user to see.

2. Long integers: these long integers are going to hold longer integer values as the name suggests. The size of a long integer is going to have the option of being as big as the memory bank that the system is currently using.

You have to remember that someone who is not a programmer will not see any difference between these two integer types and any conversions that are done between them. Not only that, but the interpreter is going to cover any conversions that must be done so that the user of your program does not have to know what a long integer is and how bit it can be.

3. Booleans: the Boolean is going to represent a true and false value. For the Boolean type, there are going to be subtypes that are used for the integers. The values of true and false are going to be similar to how the values of zero and one are going to behave when it is being converted into a string.

Example

E = 1

L = true

E + L

3

E = 4

L = false

E + L

2

L == 0

True

E == 1

True

Str (true)

Print true

Str (false)

False

4. Float: floats are only going to double the precision of float point numbers. You will see these used in machine architecture or whenever they have to specifically be implemented by Python in order to figure out what range is accepted by the program as well as how the overflow has to be handled. Therefore, CPython is going to be limited in what it can do because it is

written in the C language. The same thing is going to happen should you be using Jython since it is written in Java.

5. Complex numbers: a complex number is going to be similar to the floating-point numbers. The same rules are going to be implemented to complex numbers. You will have the option of creating a complex number by using the complex keyword.

Example

Complex (4, 5)

(4 + 5j)

You will use the literal prefix of j when you are working with complex numbers. You always have the option of using the complex z to get into the attributes that are read only. When doing this, you are going to use z.real for the real numbers and z.imag for the imaginary ones.

Mapping

When doing the mapping in Python, you are going to have a finite set of values that will be placed into an immutable key. Key mappings must be hashable. Expressions such as a[k] will be used in selecting indexes with the k key. A is going to be used for assignments and del for delete statements. You can also use dict for the dictionary expressions.

1. Dictionary: a dictionary is going to be key-value pairs that are separated by commas placed within a set of braces. You can also use the constructor of dict( ). One of the primary operations that you will see supported by this type is going to be values that are selected, deleted,

and added with the key that has been assigned to that action. Whenever you must add keys that have already been put into the dict, the older value is going to be forgotten.

As you try to access the values by using a key that does not exist, you will end up getting a key error exception. The dictionaries may very well be considered one of the most important types that can be found inside of the interpreter. If you did not have the dictionary made in your interpreter, one is going to be made by default inside of the interpreter when numbers are put into different places.

Since Python is ever evolving, there are going to be more advanced forms of the dictionary type that can be used in Python and they are known as collections. In order to bring a collection into a dictionary, you will use the OrderdDict technique so that the order of the items that are in your default dict are remembered and moved over. Should a key be missing, then Python is going to produce a value for that key which will then update your key pair with the value that was created.

Example

Python

The collections will be imported with the default dict

Z = defaultdict (int)

Z

Defaultdict (<class 'nit'>, { })

Z [7]

0

Z

Defaultdict (<class 'nit'>, { 7: 0}

Callable types

The callable types are going to be the data types that you are going to be able to use when needing to support the function call operation. You are going to invoke the call operation by using a set of parentheses.

Example

Def print_cat (cat):

Print (cat)

However, a function is not the only thing that can be called on when you are working in Python. You are able to call on any object type by using the _call_ script. Whenever a function that has been called is checked, then it is going to be deemed as a callable function. There are four different types of callable functions that have been built into Python. Each of which you saw in the beginner's book.

As a recap, the callable function types are classes, functions that have been built into Python, user defined functions, and methods.

CHAPTER 2: OBJECT ORIENTED PROGRAMMING

A class is going to be based on a program that is object oriented. These classes are one of the more basic organizational units that can be found inside of Python.

Class definitions – the mechanics

Whenever you use the class statement, you are going to be defining a new class type. Each class statement is going to be used to define variables, methods, and attributes that are all going to be associated with the collection.

Example

Class finances (element) :

Num_finances = 0

Def _int_ (own, title, balance) :

Own. Title = title

Own. Balance = balance

Finacnes.num_finances += 1

Def del_finances (own) :

Finances. Num_finances -=1

Def insert (own, amount) :

Own. Balance = own. Balance

Def output (own, amount)

Own balance = own balance

Def search (own)

Return own. Balance

A class definition will introduce a class object which will either fall in as a method object or an instance object.

Class objects

As a class statement is carried out, a class object is going to be created. Whenever the execution process is started, there is going to be a new namespace that is made where all the attributes for the class are going to go. You will notice that unlike with Java, there is not going to be a new local scope that is created just so that the class method can be used.

In the above example, you will notice that the finances class is going to show you how the namespace works. The technique that is being used is the num_finances variable, and because of how Python operates, you are going to have to use this since it is a fully qualified name. If you were to use something like finances.num_finances then an error would be displayed on your screen since you did not use the qualified name.

Example

Num_finances = 0

Def _int_ (own, title, balance) :

Own. Title = title

Own. Balance = balance

Finacnes.num_finances += 1

Def del_finances (own) :

Finances. Num_finances -=1

Def insert (own, amount) :

Own. Balance = own. Balance

Def output (own, amount)

Own balance = own balance

Def search (own)

Return own. Balance

Finances = finance ('ele', 20)

Traceback to the last call used

File Python line 1 in <module>

File Python line 2 in _init_

Unboundlocalerror: the local variable for 'num_finances' is referenced before the assignment.

After everything has been executed from the class statement, the class object will be created, a scope that comes before the class' definition is going to put back into the code so that the object becomes bound to the scope and the class name that was identified inside of the class definition.

You do not have to stick to just one class, though. You do have the ability to use some diversity. Sticking with how Python thinks, every value that is placed in Python is going to be an object. And every object will have a class which will be created with the type class method.

While it is not going to make much sense, a class is going to have its own class that works behind it.

Example

Class_name = finances

Class_parents = (element)

Class_body = " " "

Num_finances = 0

Def _int_ (own, title, balance) :

Own. Title = title

Own. Balance = balance

Finacnes.num_finances += 1

Def del_finances (own) :

Finances. Num_finances -=1

Def insert (own, amount) :

Own. Balance = own. Balance

Def output (own, amount)

Own balance = own balance

Def search (own)

Return own. Balance

" " "

#new dicts will be used by the local name space

Class_dict = { }

the class body will be carried out with the name space.

Exec (class_body, world ( ), class_dict)

looking at the class dict will show the name binding created from the class body.

Etc.

As the class statement is carried out, your interpreter is going to do a kind of carries which is going to follow these steps.

1. The class statement body will become isolated into a class object.
2. The dictionary for the class is going to be shown by a namespace that is created by the class.
3. Your object code that represents the body of the class will be carried out inside of its namespace only.
4. It is during this last step that we will discover that the object is created through the type class. It will have to

go through the type class so that the base classes and the dictionary can be created based on the types arguments. Meta classes are going to also be used in creating class objects which can be set specifically to the metaclass through the metaclass argument being placed into the class definition. Should it not be supplied, then the default type is going to be invoked.

A class object is going to support the object instantiation and the attribute reference. These attributes are going to be referenced through the use of a dot syntax in which the object will be followed by a dot and then the name of the attribute. When you have a valid attribute name, the variable and method names are going to be seen in the classes namespace after the class has been created.

Example

Financial.num_financial

0

Financial.insert

<unbound method financial method financial.insert>

Object instantiation is going to be executed by calling the class objects as you would a normal function that has the parameters set up as they should be.

Example

Financial ("ele", 0)

These instance objects will be invoked through the use of an argument that will be given to it after the class object is returned. Whenever you look at the financial class, the financial name and the balance are going to be set and will increase in one integer increments because of the _init_ method.

Instance objects

If the class objects were to be cookie cutters and your instances were the cookies that you were cooking, then after you cook those cookies, you are going to get an instantiating class object. These objects will be returned once the proper initialization for that class.

The attribute reference will be the single operation that is valid when working with an instance object. The attributes for the instance are known as instance variables when you are working with other programming languages such as Java. You may also hear them called instance variables or method attributes.

Method objects

In the event that L is the instance of the financial class, it is going to mean that the method object is L. input. A method object is going to be similar to the function that is being used when the method is being defined. There is another argument that will need to be included in the argument list known as the self-argument. With this new argument, you are going to get the instance referring to the class. However, why is the instance being pass off as an argument in this method?

Example

L = financial ( )

L. search ( )

20

At the point in time that the instance method is called on, you will see it being done by the L. inquiry ( ) method. It is this method that is going to call without having to use the argument you saw in the example above despite the method being defined with inquiry ( ). The inquiry method is going to rely on having the self-argument.

If you observe the example shown above, you are going to see that the call is done on L. search ( ) which is going to be the equivalent of having written out financial. Search (L). Take notice that the instance of L is going through the argument in order to get to the method which will be the self-argument. By invoking this method, the argument list will become equivalent to as if you were to force the corresponding method to start by using the method's object. In an effort to see how this is going to work, you will be able to notice that the methods are going to be stored inside of the class dicts as a function.

 Example

Type (financial. Search)

<class 'func'>

Everything changed in a short period of time! To understand how this happened, you need to understand what is happening with the attribute references and the descriptors that are inside of the Python code.

In essence, your method object is going to curl around your function object which in turn is going to cause the argument list to be called and a new argument list to be started with that underlying function's object. You are going to see that this is going to be applied to every instance method even if you are using the _init_ method. Keep in mind that the self-argument will not be the true keyword, this word is simply a convention for a valid argument name that is going to be able to be used for the class definition.

Example

Class Financial (element) :

Num_financial = 2

Class_name = finances

Class_parents = (element)

Class_body = " " "

Num_finances = 0

Def _int_ (own, title, balance) :

Own. Title = title

Own. Balance = balance

Finances.num_finances += 1

Def del_finances (own) :

Finances. Num_finances -=1

Def insert (own, amount) :

Own. Balance = own. Balance

Def output (own, amount)

Own balance = own balance

Def search (own)

Return own. Balance

Financial. Num_financial

2

L = financial ('ele', 2)

L. insert (30)

Financial. Search (L)

30

Customizing the types that are defined by the user

At this point you should have a good feel for Python and know that it is a language that is flexible, and that is going to work towards doing what the user wants rather than the program developers since not everyone is going to be on the same page as far as what they are trying to get out of their coding. Python offers its users the ability to take their classes and modify them to where they would not be able to if they were using another programming language. The class creation, initialization of the object, and the access the function will have to the attribute are just a few of the ways that you can modify your code to fit what you are wanting to be done. A type that is defined by the user can also be customized in order to change how it is going to behave. It can be changed to behave more like a type that is built into the program as well as have the option of supporting syntax and special operators.

Despite the fact that you can customize to your heart's content, this makes the method known as a special or a magic method. These special methods are normal methods; they are going to be set off by double underscores as well as be followed by these underscores. A special method that you have most likely been using this entire time is the _init_ method that you are using to initialize the instance for the class. Another that you may have used is the _getitem_ that is going to be a method invoked by the index; these indexes are going to be things such as L [p] which will then be given over to the interpreter to translate and execute.

When you see methods that have the double underscore before and after the name, you will be working with a method that is normal for Python, the only difference is that you can customize it to what you want it to do therefore making it to where you are going to need to approach using these methods differently after they have been customized.

The user-defined classes can also be implemented through the use of a special method known as the corollary. This operator is built into Python and uses the plus symbol and the square brackets. Every class that can be defined by the user will be able to use these symbols. It is essential to know that corollary is a big part of polymorphism.

Special methods used with instance creation

Both the _init_ and _new_ functions are going to be special methods that are going to have two ways that they can be used when it comes to instance creation. A new class instance is going to be done through the use of a two-step process.

The static method is going to be when you use the _new_ method and create a brand-new class before turning around and initiating the _init_ method so that new object can be initialized with the arguments that have been provided.

It is of vital importance that you recognize when you should override the _new_ method, and that will be when you are trying to sub class an immutable type that has been built into the program. Any initialization that is completed by this sub class has to be done before your object creation is done. This is done so that you are sure that you have the proper object created due to the fact that once it is created, it will become immutable. Therefore, you should never try to carry out a function that is not able to be changed because you put the wrong objects into it.

Example

Import arithmetic

Class following integer (int) :

Def _new_ (class, value) :

Return int. _new_ (class, arithmetic, ceil (value following integer (3.4)

4

While working with the math.ceil technique, the _init_ method is going to take that object initialization and cause it to fail. Your _new_ method is going to be able to be overridden so that a superclass is created and all the sub classes under it are going to contain a single instance during the entire execution of the program.

Example

Class single

Def _new_ (class *argument, **kwds):

It = class. _dict_ . get ("_element_")

Should it be returned it is none :

Return the element

Class. _element_ = element = item. _new_ (class)

It.init (*arg, **kwds)

Return element

Def _init_ (own, *args, **kwsds) :

Pass

You should take note that when you are implemented that _new_ method and through that implementation you will be creating a base class which will cause that implementation to return an object.

If you are already familiar with defining the _init_ method, then this method can be used in order to override the performance attributes that belong to the instances of mutable types.

Special method for attribute access

A special method is going to allow the tools that you are going to need to customize the attribute references. It is these tools that are going to allow you to have access and to set that attribute once you have customized it.

1. _getattr_: you can implement this method as an effort to handle a situation where an attribute that has been referenced cannot be found. With this method, you can only call on it whenever your attribute is not an instance or because it cannot be found inside of your class tree for that particular object. You will get a value returned for your attribute, or you are going to get an attribute error exception that is going to be displayed on your screen.

Example

Class_name = finances

Class_parents = (element)

Class_body = " " "

Num_finances = 0

Def _int_ (own, title, balance) :

Own. Title = title

Own. Balance = balance

Finacnes.num_finances += 1

Def del_finances (own) :

Def _getattr_ (own, title):

Return : no attribute called { }. Format (title)

Finances. Num_finances -=1

Def insert (own, amount) :

Own. Balance = own. Balance

Def output (own, amount)

Own balance = own balance

Def search (own)

Return "title = { }, balance, = { }" format (own .title, own balance)

L = financial ('ele', 3)

L. financial

No attributes have been called by the name of financial.

You have to be careful with the implementation for _getattr_ due to the fact that the implementation references for the attribute instance are not going to exist which is then going to cause an infinite loop to occur.

2. _getattribute_: you are going to be implementing the customization of your attribute so that it can access a class. The use of this method is always going to be called unconditionally whenever you are accessing the attribute for the instance in that class.
3. _setattr_: this method will start to implement the attribute assignment that is unconditional. This method should only be placed on the value that is being assigned into the dictionary for that attribute rather than to us a different code which is going to cause you to get an infinite recursive call. _setattr_( ) will be used whenever the attribute instance assignment needs it to be. Your base class method is going to use the same name, and in using it, the code will look like this: super ( ) _setattr_ (self, title, amount).

CHAPTER 3: FUNCTIONS

Functions are going to be named or anonymous statements and expressions. With Python, the functions in Python are going to be first class objects. So, there is not going to be any restriction your functions and what values you use. Introspection is going to have the ability to be carried out on your function. Your function can also be assigned to the variables or used an argument.

Function definition

Your def keyword is going to create a user defined function which will then be executed. If you were to take a function definition such as the square root, then the function is only going to use the def square (a) to execute the definition of that function.

The anonymous function that will be created with the use of the lambda keyword.

Example lambda_stat :: = "lambda, [argument _ list] : statement

This lambda function is going to return a function object to you once it has been evaluated. There may be some of the same attributes that are going to be named for the functions. The lambda express is typically going to be used when working with simple functions since the lambda definition is going to be able to deal with a single expression.

Example

Square = lambda L : L * * 2

For x in range (8)

Square (x)

0, 1, 4

Functions and objects

A function is going to have values that are going to be labeled as objects, and these objects are going to have the function type.

Example def square (a)   ⁴

Return a*a

Type (square)

<class 'fun'>

And, just like every object in Python, functions are going to use the dir () function in order to show what all of the attributes are for that function.

A few of the most important attributes that you will use with your function are.

1. _annotations_: the attribute is going to have metadata this is optional for the arguments and any return types that will be given to the function's definition.

Example

Def square (a : int) - >

Return a * a

Square. _annotations)

{'a' : <class 'nite>, 'return' : <class 'nit'>}

Any parameters that you have to use will be annotated by colons which are going to be located at the end of the parameters name. After the parameter has been evaluated in order to figure out what the value is going to be the annotated through the use of a literal. This literal will to be followed by the expression that has been placed between your parameter lists and the ending colon.

1. _doc_: the documentation string is going to be returned to your function

Example

Def square (a):

The square of any number you want will be given.

Return a ** 2

Square. _doc_

The square that is returned is going to be the square of a number.

2. _name_: the function name is going to be returned
Square.func_name

Square

3. _module_: the name of the module is going to be defined

Example

Square. _module_

primary

4. _defaults_: a tuple is going to be returned with the values that are automatically set for that tuple.
5. _kwdefaults_: the dict is going to have the keyword arguments that are default for Python
6. _globals_: references will be made to the diction where all of the functions are going to be held.

Square. Function_world

{ '_already in_' : <module '_alreadyin_' (built in)> '_title_' '_primary_', 'square' : < funct \ n square at 0x131542c92> '_doc_' : nothing, '_package_' : nothing}

7. _dict_: your names spaces are going to be returned in order to support the function attributes

Square. Function_dict

{ }

8. _closure_: a tuple is going to be retuned with the cells that bind everything in the free variables for the function.

Most functions are going to have to be passed through the argument to other functions, and the function that takes on another function will be known as a higher-order functional program.

Example

Map (square, distance (4)

[0, 1, 4]

Functions can also be defined even if they are located in another function which will then return a function call.

Example

Def create _ number ():

Count = 2

Def count ( ) :

Nonlocal amount # this will capture the number of times that the bind gets out of the scope, but it is not going to matter about the global scope.

Count += 3

Return count

Return opposite.

Descriptors

Functions also have the capabilities of being a descriptor. We are going to look a little closer at the attributes for functions. With this function, you are going to be using the _get_ method to make the function a non-data descriptor.

Example

Def square (a) :

Outcome a ** 2

Dir (square) # use the _get_ attribute

[_annotation_, _call_, _class_, _closed_,

...

By using the _get_ method, whenever you call on it, the function is going to be referenced and then will display the mechanics that you will use in order to handle the method call for the objects and the normal function calls. The characteristics of the descriptor for functions will always enable the function to be returned back to itself or to a method that is bound depending on where and how the function has been referenced.

CHAPTER 4: ITERATOR IN PYTHON

An iterable that can be found in Python is going to technically be any object that has the option of implementing the _iter_ method. Whenever the returns are called on, the iterator is going to be invoked so that the iter (element) method is put into place.

Essentially, the program has the option of putting an iterable into any type that is using a 'for' 'in' loop. This is going to be a list, tuple, set, or dict that will be able to have objects that have been iterated. The iterator protocol is going to be started because of the iterator objects. The protocol states that these methods are going to be used in the implementation process for any object that is going to be used as an iterator.

1. _iter_: the method is going to start the iterator and is always going to return the _next_ function to you.
2. _next_: here you are going to be calling the next () global function. Once it has been found, then it will be invoked with the iterator for the arguments that are going to be used. It is also the _next_ method that is going to be used in the 'for' 'in' look just like the last implementation. When using it with the 'for' look, the next () iterator is going to be called on. It is this method that is going to raise the stop iterator exception where you do not have to have a new value returned to you at the end of the iteration.

Keep in mind to take care when it comes to telling the iterable and the iterator apart due to the fact that the iterable is not going to always e your iterator.

Example

A = [2, 4, 5]

Type (a)

<class 'tuple'>

A_iter = iter (a)

<class 'tuple_iterator'>

#a is not an iterable and is not go to be used for a loop.

Dir (a)

[_add_, _class_ etc]

One thing you should know is that many times the iterable objects are also going to have the ability to be an iterator in order to allow it to be called on by the _iter_ method. This will make I to where the method is returned to the object itself.

Classes that implement the iterator protocol fully are going to be used as iterators. You can see this in the Fibonacci sequence.

Example

Class fib

Def _init_ (own, total) :

Own. Total = total

Def _iter_ (own) : own. L = 2 own. E =2 return own

Objects are iterable and an iterator as well

Def _next_ (own) :

Fib = own. L

If fib > own. Total

Top iteration

Own. L own e = own e own l + own e

Return fib

For L in fib (20):

Print L

Setting up a range that is customized is going to primarily be done when it comes to loops with numbers that are going to be modeled as iterators.

Example

Class customized :

Def _init_ (own, total):

Own. Current = 2

Return own

Def _next_ (own) :

Amount = own. Current

If own. Current >= own. Total:

Raise stop iteration

Own. Current += 2

Return amount

For L in customized (30)

Print L

0, 1, 2, 3, 4, 5, 6, 7, 8, 9

Before you are able to go to the next step, you are going to want to stop and look at both of the examples that you were just shown. To make it easy to understand, your iterator that is going to be the iterator object will be used in calculating and returning elements that are inside of a sequence as it is needed instead of doing it all at once.

Your custom range is not going to give you every element that is inside of the range after it has been initialized; instead, it is going to give you objects whenever they are called on by the _iter_ method. From there you are going to only get the iterator objects that will have the ability to calculate what the next element in your range is going to be. Python will be following the steps that the _next_ method uses to complete this process.

You can define your range to make it to where all of them return only positive whole numbers by taking out the upper bound on your method. The same is going to apply when it comes to using the fib iterator.

You can look at Python and see that the functions that are built in are going to return sequences.

Example

The range function is not going to give you a list as an outcome because you are going to have to be at a more advanced level than where you are. However, the object that is returned in the range for the iterator object is while using the _iter_ method. The sequence is going to expect that the range iterator is going to be passed on to the list of constructors.

Your iterator protocol is going to start a form of computing that you are going to learn is called the lazy computation. It is not going to do more work than it has to at one time so if you are wanting your equation to be calculated quickly the lazy computation is not going to be the way that you are going to want to go.

Itertools module

Python has a module that is going to work with iterators which is known as the itertools module. This module is going to give some of the general-purpose functions that are going to give you an outcome of an iterator. Whenever you get these results, you are going to be getting them by passing your iterator that you return to your list () constructor.

These are some of the functions that you may get:

1. Accumulate (iterable [, func]: an iterable along with the function argument will be added into the operator.add function. IF you do not supply a function, then the default one is going to take two arguments and give you just one value. Elements for the iterable have to be one of the types that Python accepts in the supplied function. Calling will cause an accumulated return of the iterator while representing the result of what your

applying the supplied function and element of the iterable. Any accumulated results are for the first element will be the element itself while the result is going to be the nth element of the code fun(nth element, accumulated result of (n-1)th element.)

Example

From itertools import

Gather ([3, 5, 2, 5, 6,])

Itertools. Gather element

List (gather ([3, 5, 2, 5, 6]))

[9, 25, 4, 25, 36]

Import operator

Gather (range (4, 2) operator. Mul)

Etc.

2. Chain(*iterable): a single iterable is going to hold a variable number for iterable and then give you an iterator that is showing the union for all of the iterable that have been placed inside the iterable that has been supplied.
3. Combinations (iterable, r): an outcome of an iterator that is going to show the set of R's subsequence length for the elements that are inside of the iterable that was inputted. Elements that will be given special treatment because of their value rather than their position.
4. Groupby (iterable, key = None): an iterator will be returned before the following keys are returned along

with the corresponding groups that are going to tie those iterable arguments together. The key argument is going to be the function that calculated the key value of every element. Should a key function not be assigned as a value or none, then there is going to be a key element that will automatically default so that the function can be returned and the element is unchanged. Typically, the iterable is going to be sorted according to the key function. But, the group that is returned will be returned as an iterator that is going to share the iterable that is laying under the iterator along with groupby ().

5. I slice(terable, start, stop [, step]) : your iterator is going to be returning elements that are from your iterable but only inside of a specific range of numbers. Should your start be a non-zero element, then every other element is going to be skipped until the start is found. Once the start has been found, the elements are going to be returned in order according to the step elements. This means that if a step is greater than another step, it will be skipped by using a slice. This is going to be done until the iterable argument can no longer be met. However, unlike the slicing you are used to, I slice () is not going to allow you to use negative values for any of your starts, stops, or steps.

6. Permutation(iterable, r = none) : the succession of your r length will be returned permutations of the elements that are in your iterable. In the event that r is not specified or is set to none, then the default will be used for the iterable length. Elements in this function are going to be treated like they are unique because of what position they occupy rather than what their value is as well as where their permutations are different from any combination that has already been defined. Therefore, if the input is going to be unique, that means there is not going to be values that will repeat based on every permutation that occurs.

7. Product (*iterable, repeat = 1): the iterator will be returned in succession according to the Cartesian product for input iterable. This is going to be a lot like using a 'for' loop that has been nested into a list. It is this function that you are going to be able to compute the product for an iterable within itself through the specification of the number of times you want it to repeat with that optional keyword argument.

CHAPTER 5: PYTHON GENERATORS

Generators are kind of the same thing as an iterator, and it is going to work very closely with iterators so that you are getting the answer that you need when it comes to your code.

In Python, generators are known as generator- iterators, and it is generators that will generate (just like the name says) the values whenever the _next_ method has been called. A generator is going to be used whenever you are specifically calling the _next_ method or when you are using a generator object inside of a 'for' 'in' loop.

There are two types of generators you will be working within Python. Generator expressions and generator functions.

Functions of generators

The generator functions are going to be the functions that hold the yield expression. Whenever you call a function that contains this expression, you are going to be getting a generator object returned to you.

Example

Def fib (full):

E, a = 9, 2

While e < full:

Yield e

E, a = a, e + a

The yield keyword

The syntax for the yield keyword is:

Yield expression_list

Your yield keyword is going to be the expression that is going to be tied to the generator functions. In order to truly understand what the yield expression does, you have to compare it to the return keyword. Return is going to be encountered whenever the control of the function needs to be returned to the caller so that the function is terminated.

Example

Def fib (full):

Amounts = [ ]

L, e = 9, 4

While L < full:

Amounts.appened (L)

L, e = e, L + e

Return numbers

here is where your values are going to be returned to you all at once.

With that being said, if you introduce the yield expression into that function, it is going to go from being simple to understand to being more complex. Functions that have the yield expression that has been called are not going to work as a regular expression does. Instead, it is going to give you a generator expression.

Example

F = fib (43)

F

<generator's object fib at 0x2394a4482>

Generator objects are going to be carried out when the _next_ method becomes invoked which causes all of the generator objects to execute every statement that has been found inside of the function definition until the yield keyword stops it.

Example

e. _next_ ( )

3

E _next_ ( )

4

E _next_ ( )

4

F _next_ ( )
9

Objects will suspend the execution during any part of its process in order to save the context and return a value in the expression list for your caller. Now, when the call puts the _next_ ( ) method into action, the function will be executed once again until it hits another yield or return or even if the end of the function is reached. Your function is going to keep doing this until the condition is found to be false which will put a stop iteration exception up in your code.

PEP 255 states:

"If a yield statement is encountered, the state of the function is frozen, and the value of expression_list is returned to._nex_ ( )'s caller. By "frozen" we mean that all local state is retained, including the current bindings of local variables, the instruction pointer, and the internal evaluation stack: enough information is saved so that the next time next ( ) is invoked, the function can proceed exactly as if the yield statement were just another external call. On the other hand, when a function encounters a return statement, it returns to the caller along with any value proceeding the return statement and the execution of such function is complete for all intent and purposes. One can think of yield as causing only a temporary interruption in the execution of a function."

Now that you understand generators a little more, you can most likely now see how the generators are going to be used in order to implement the iterator. Many generators have been known to calculate the next value that will fall in the sequence to ensure that the function will return the iterator so that it can be rewritten by using the yield statement. In order to show you what this means, the accumulator function that can be found in the itertools module will be rewritten by using generators.

Example

Def gather (iterable, function = operator. Insert) :

'running totals will be returned.'

gather ([3, 4, 5, 6]) → 7, 9, 11

gather ([3, 5, 6, 7]) , the operators.mul)

It = iter (iterable)

Attempt

Full = next (it)

Do not include stop iteration

Return

Yield complete

For an object in it:

Complete = func (complete, object)

Yield complete

Just like you have the option of emulating a generated object through the use of implementing the iterator protocol, you can also use the yield keyword in order to get a more succinct method that will be used for the creation of generators.

Generator expressions

One of the biggest issues that you are going to find when you are using list comprehension is that the values are all going to have to be calculated at once even if you are not using them right then or ever. This is going to often times take up more room than what needs to be taken up on the memory of the computer. The PEP 289 had proposed that the generator expression is going to be able to resolve this and when it was accepted and added to the language to see if it was the fix that they needed.

Generator expressions are going to work similarly to list comprehensions; however, the list comprehension square brackets are going to be replaced with a set of parentheses so that you get an outcome that will be your generator expression object.

Example

Generating a list for the square of the numbers 2-8:

Squares = [a * 2 for a in range (8)]

Squares

the square root for numbers 2 through 8 will be printed here.

Now a generator expression is going to take the place of the list comprehension

Squares = [a * 2 for a in range (8)]

Squares

<generator object <genexpr> at 0x2940d9s94>

You are going to be able to access the values for your generator by using the _next_ ( ) or a 'for' 'in' loop.

Example

Squares = [a * 2 for a in range (8)]

For square in squares:

Print (squares)

the squares are going to be printed here

When you are using a generator expression, you will be creating a generator object without having to use the yield expression.

Iterators and generators

Generators are going to be best whenever you are working with large amounts of data. You should try and remember that you are going to want to stick with prime numbers if you can. The method that is used for calculating the set will be the Sieve of Eratosthenes.

In the following example, you are going to see that all the prime numbers will have to be less than or equal to an integer (e)

Erathosthene's method:

1. Make a list of consecutive integers from your chosen number all the way to the nth number.
2. All for t to be set as equal to your first number which will be your first prime number.

3. Starting from that first prime number, you will enumerate all of the multiples by counting up to n in increment of your first prime number be sure to mark them inside of your list. Your first prime number will not be listed.

4. Locate the first number that is greater than your variable of t in your list. But, it cannot be marked. Should there be no number, you are going to have to stop. Otherwise, you will allow t to be equal to this new number. This number is going to be your next prime number, and you will start over again at number three.

At the point in time that the algorithm is terminated, the numbers that remain are not going to be marked on the list when all the primes fall below n.

Example

From itertools bring in count

Def primes_to (general, highest value):

For I inside rang (highest value):

Print (general._next_ ( ))

Def sort_multiples_of_n (n, ints):

#in will be a generator that has the capabilities of having other generators inside of it.

For I in ints:

If (I % n) ! = 3

Yield I

Def sieve (ints):

While correct

Prime = ints. _next_ ()

Yield prime

the ints is now going to be considered a generator that will produce other generators that are multiples of your prime number

Ints = sort_multiples_of_n (prime, ints)

all the prime numbers need to be less than 100

Primes_to (shift(amount(3)) , 20)

your outcome is going to be printed here.

While it may not seem like it, the example you just saw is going to show how simple the generators can be when they are chained together through the output of one thing that you inputted. An easy way to think of it is that you are going to be stacking generators inside of one another creating something that is going to be like a pipeline.

Your function filter_multiples_of_n is going to be what initializes the generator to return the sequence of numbers that you need to have returned.

Prime = ints. _next_ ( ) will return your number to the first iteration. Once the yield expression is executed, then the ints = filter_multiples_of_n (number, ints) function is going to be invoked so that a generator is created. This generator is going to create a return that is a stream of numbers that are not multiples of the number that you have set in your function. You need to keep in mind that your original sequence is going to be captured in this new generator. Do not forget this because it is very important!

Looking at the iteration of your loop that is inside of your sieve function, your generator is going to be invoked. The loop for the generator is going to be looped through the original sequence at this point in time so that you get a number that is first in that sequence that is not going to be divisible by the number in your function or your prime number.

The prime number that is first in your sequence is going to be coming from that yield that was done on the sieve function before another generator gives you the outcome of the nonmultiples of your prime number which will then assign it to the ints.

It is this generator that is going to take the previous generator and give you the nonmultiples of the number that you used in your function. This generator is going to produce a sequence of infinite sequence of numbers. A call will be invoked with the _next_ ( ) method for the generator to loop it through the generator before it before getting the nonmultiples return. The divisibility of your first prime number is going to be checked because you are not going to want numbers that are divisible by this number to be on your list due to the fact it will be yielded.

Tying your generators together will continue to go until every number that is in your generator has been evaluated and processed or until the condition is found to be false.

The data that is moving through the different generators is going to be able to be applied to the space that is left over so that it becomes more time efficient due to the fact that you are dealing with so much data. Not only that, but the data has to go through the log files and the data bases. A generator is going to be the best way to make this easier not only for you but the program as well.

CONCLUSION

Thank you for making it through to the end of *Python Intermediate*, let's hope it was informative and able to provide you with all of the tools you need to achieve your goals whatever it may be.

The next step is to up your knowledge level! You have learned the basics and now you have a decent understanding of some of the next level of what you should be learning is going to be like.

The more that you practice, the easier it is going to be for you to understand Python. Not only that, but you will advance to more complex codes.

Finally, if you found this book useful in any way, a review on Amazon is always appreciated!

Thank you and good luck!

OTHER BOOKS BY MICHAEL KNAPP

1) : Python For Beginners: Learn the Fundamentals of Python in 7 Days

2) Python For Intermediates: Learn the Fundamentals of Python in 7 Days

3) Python For Advanced: Learn the Fundamentals of Python in 7 Days

DID YOU ENJOY THIS BOOK?

I want to thank you for purchasing and reading this book. I really hope you got a lot out of it.

Can I ask a quick favor though?

If you enjoyed this book I would really appreciate it if you could leave me a positive review on Amazon.

I love getting feedback from my customers and reviews on Amazon really do make a difference. I read all my reviews and would really appreciate your thoughts.

Thanks so much.

Michael Knapp

Made in the USA
San Bernardino, CA
15 August 2017